INSIDE COLLEGE FOOTBALL

FLORIDA GATORS

BY TONY HUNTER

abdobooks.com

Published by Abdo Publishing, a division of ABDO, PO Box 398166, Minneapolis, Minnesota 55439. Copyright © 2021 by Abdo Consulting Group, Inc. International copyrights reserved in all countries. No part of this book may be reproduced in any form without written permission from the publisher. SportsZone™ is a trademark and logo of Abdo Publishing.

Printed in the United States of America, North Mankato, Minnesota
022020
092020

THIS BOOK CONTAINS RECYCLED MATERIALS

Cover Photo: John Raoux/AP Images
Interior Photos: Paul Spinelli/AP Images, 5; Charles Krupa/AP Images, 8; Courtesy of the State Archives of Florida, 11; John Lindsay/AP Images, 15; HC/AP Images, 17; James Drake/Sports Illustrated/Set Number: X12007/Getty Images, 19; Sporting News Archive/Sporting News/Getty Images, 22; Collegiate Images/Getty Images, 25, 43; AP Images, 27; Scott Halleran/Allsport/Getty Images Sport/Getty Images, 29; Dave Martin/AP Images, 30; Chris O'Meara/AP Images, 33; John Bazemore/AP Images, 34; John Raoux/AP Images, 36; Matthew Stamey/AP Images, 40

Editor: Patrick Donnelly
Series Designer: Nikki Nordby

Library of Congress Control Number: 2019954376

Publisher's Cataloging-in-Publication Data

Names: Hunter, Tony, author.
Title: Florida Gators / by Tony Hunter
Description: Minneapolis, Minnesota : Abdo Publishing, 2021 | Series: Inside college football | Includes online resources and index.
Identifiers: ISBN 9781532192425 (lib. bdg.) | ISBN 9781098210328 (ebook)
Subjects: LCSH: Florida Gators (Football team)--Juvenile literature. | Universities and colleges--Athletics--Juvenile literature. | American football--Juvenile literature. | College sports--United States--History--Juvenile literature.
Classification: DDC 796.33263--dc23

TABLE OF CONTENTS

CHAPTER 1
**RUNNING AWAY
WITH A CROWN**........................ 4

CHAPTER 2
THE GROWING GATORS........... 10

CHAPTER 3
**PUTTING FLORIDA
FOOTBALL ON THE MAP**.......... 16

CHAPTER 4
**GRIDIRON GREATS
IN GAINESVILLE**...................... 24

CHAPTER 5
THE CHAMPIONSHIP ERA......... 32

TIMELINE	42
QUICK STATS	44
QUOTES AND ANECDOTES	45
GLOSSARY	46
MORE INFORMATION	47
ONLINE RESOURCES	47
INDEX	48
ABOUT THE AUTHOR	48

CHAPTER 1

RUNNING AWAY WITH A CROWN

The University of Florida Gators football team was preparing to face the Ohio State Buckeyes in the 2006 Bowl Championship Series (BCS) National Championship Game. The showdown was set for January 8, 2007.

Gators head coach Urban Meyer had an idea for motivating his players. He placed a huge bulletin board in the locker room during the week before the game. On it, he posted articles written about the team. Some articles predicted Ohio State would easily win. Others featured so-called experts claiming the Gators could not match up to the talented Buckeyes.

Meyer later referred to the board as "10 feet of nonsense." That's because some items he placed on it were pure fiction. They were created simply to upset his players. His plan was a huge success. The players grew angrier as the showdown approached.

Urban Meyer led Florida to the 2006 national championship game in just his second year as the Gators' coach.

OHIO'S OWN

Urban Meyer led Florida to the 2006 national title over the team he rooted for when he was growing up. Meyer was born and raised in Ohio. In fact, when he was younger, he hoped to someday play for the Buckeyes.

Meyer grew up in the town of Ashtabula, Ohio. He starred in baseball. Meyer's father was often demanding and emphasized athletic success. Once when he was a senior in high school, Meyer played a brilliant game as both a hitter and a fielder. But Meyer made an out in the last inning. His father was so mad he made Meyer run the 5 miles (8 km) home.

Meyer eventually accomplished his dream of coaching the Buckeyes. He left Florida in 2010 and was hired by Ohio State in 2011. Meyer led the Buckeyes to three Big Ten titles and a national title in 2014. He retired from coaching after the 2018 season but remained working in the Ohio State athletics department in addition to becoming a broadcaster.

Meyer worked to make the Gators believe they were better than Ohio State.

Florida proved it was worthy throughout the year. The Gators play in the Southeastern Conference (SEC). Many considered it to be the toughest football conference in 2006. Florida was one of six SEC teams ranked among the nation's top 25 in the final poll that season. The Gators beat four of the other five. Florida's only loss came against the Auburn Tigers. Auburn finished the season ranked ninth.

Gators junior defensive end Jarvis Moss required no convincing. "We were such a tight team and had our own identity," he said. "We knew who we were and what Ohio State was. Our coaches didn't have to convince us we could beat Ohio State. I think everybody on our team knew we were better than Ohio State and faster than them before we even played the game."

Ohio State did have one speedy player who could give the Gators problems. Wide receiver Ted Ginn Jr. showed off that speed on the opening kickoff. Ginn returned it 93 yards for a touchdown.

Meyer believed his team needed to answer with a touchdown on the next drive. And that is what the Gators did. Senior quarterback Chris Leak threw a touchdown pass to senior wide receiver Dallas Baker to tie the game. After that, the Gators never looked back.

Standout freshman wide receiver Percy Harvin scored a touchdown on a short run just minutes later in the first quarter. And senior running back DeShawn Wynn added another touchdown on the first play of the second quarter. That stretched the Gators' lead to 21–7.

But the Buckeyes were not ready to give up. They came back four plays later with a touchdown. Then Florida responded with two field goals. And Moss took matters into his own hands. He sacked Ohio State quarterback Troy Smith, who fumbled the ball. The Gators recovered on Ohio State's 5-yard line.

Meyer sent Florida's dual-threat quarterback Tim Tebow onto the field. Then just a freshman, Tebow would eventually become an

✖ **Florida freshman quarterback Tim Tebow prepares to throw in the first half of the 2007 national championship game.**

all-time great for the Gators. But in 2006 he was mainly used in spot situations to try to confuse defenses. This time, Meyer called for a passing play. And Tebow completed a pass to junior wide receiver Andre Caldwell for the touchdown. That put Florida up 34–14 at halftime. The play capped a stunning first half against what had been a powerful defense in Ohio State.

Florida added one more touchdown in the second half. It was enough to secure a dominating 41–14 victory. After the game, Meyer held the crystal championship trophy above his head. Then he passed it to Leak. The senior planted a big kiss on the trophy. He had finished his college career as a champion. Florida was the number one team in the nation.

The college football world was stunned. Many were surprised that Florida won, let alone by 27 points. But Baker was among the many Florida players who expected a victory.

"I'm not surprised at all," he said while his teammates celebrated. "We had something to prove. Some people were predicting Ohio State to win 41–14. Well, it was 41–14 for the University of Florida.

"Nobody gave us a chance. Now, we can finally throw up a number one. We had a lot of doubters out there—the media, the Ohio State fans. No one can doubt us now. We're national champs."

GATORS GLORY

Florida beat Ohio State to become the national champions in football in January 2007. Nine months earlier, the Gators had won the men's basketball championship. The school became the first to capture the title in both sports in the same year. Three months after Florida and Ohio State faced off for the football title, the two schools faced off in the basketball championship game. Florida won this one as well, claiming back-to-back titles.

CHAPTER 2

THE GROWING GATORS

It was November 22, 1901. People throughout the United States were preparing for Thanksgiving. And the Florida Agricultural College football team was playing its first game.

The showdown was against nearby Stetson University. The *Florida Times-Union* newspaper wrote highly of the game. It referred to football as a "royal game" that tests "the best resources, the pluck, the endurance, and speed of lusty young manhood."

The game, however, was no thing of beauty. The team described during its earliest days as "the Blue and White" lost 6–0 to Stetson. The outcome might have been different had one sure touchdown pass not hit a tree stump on the field.

The school was renamed the University of Florida in 1903. It adopted the Gators nickname five years later. But those changes

The 1916 Florida Gators pose for a photograph. Florida did not achieve much success in its early years.

HITCHHIKING TO GLORY

Charlie LaPradd yearned to play for Florida. He still had that dream after surviving dangerous missions as a paratrooper in World War II. So he hitchhiked to Florida in 1949 and asked for a chance to play.

Coach Bob Woodruff provided him with an opportunity. And LaPradd blossomed into an All-American. He starred as both an offensive and defensive lineman. LaPradd is still considered one of the finest players in the history of the program.

"(He) was extremely tough," said teammate Joe D'Agostino. "It took two or three men to get him out of the way. They couldn't move him. He was our team captain, and he kept up the spirit on the line. He'd come up and down the line, hitting us on the butt and telling us to get with it and play hard, and we all loved him."

did not bring more victories. One early Florida team lost to Alabama, Auburn, Georgia, and Georgia Tech by a combined score of 201–0.

Florida joined the Southern Intercollegiate Athletic Association in 1912. The Gators had a winning record in seven of 10 years. But they finished just 0–5 in 1916, scoring only three points all season. The school yearbook staff took a more positive spin on the season: "They have the admiration and satisfaction of a loyal student body that supported them through all the trials and troubles of defeat."

A new era started in 1922 when the Gators joined the Southern Conference. In the next 11 years, Florida had eight winning seasons.

The Gators peaked in 1928, going 8–1 under coach Charlie Bachman. That year, they led the nation in scoring. Junior end Dale Van Sickel also became Florida's first All-American.

The defense shined that season. Florida gave up no more than seven points in any of its first eight games. Then it lost 13–12 against Tennessee. That loss prevented the Gators from finishing undefeated. It also prevented them from landing a berth in the Rose Bowl. The Rose Bowl is the oldest and some say most prestigious bowl game.

Florida followed that season by going 8–2 in 1929. But as the United States fell into the Great Depression, so did the Gators. They joined the SEC in 1933. And they had just one winning season from 1935 to 1951. Even then, they only finished 4–3 that year, in 1944.

The school did not make football a priority during those times. Money was tight around the country during the 1930s. Then the United States entered World War II in 1941. So many young men were fighting in Europe and Asia that Florida did not field a team in 1943.

The Gators simply could not compete during that period in the tough SEC. They had an 18–60–5 record against league opponents from 1935 to 1951. And they won no more than one SEC game in a season from 1941 to 1947. Fuller Warren was running for governor of the state in 1948. He mentioned the Gators' woes during a speech.

"Next to my pledge to try to get the cows outlawed from public highways," Warren once recalled, "my pledge to try and get that winning football team at Florida seemed to get the most applause."

The state passed a bill that sent money earned through gambling to the Florida football program. The next step was hiring 34-year-old coach Bob Woodruff away from Baylor in 1950. Woodruff demanded what was then a huge salary of $17,000 per year.

Florida did improve under Woodruff. But the team still did not win any conference or national titles. The Gators got another boost in 1950, when talented quarterback Haywood Sullivan chose to attend Florida. He threw for more than 2,000 yards in two seasons. But the Gators went just 5–5 each of those years. Then Sullivan left the school to pursue a career in Major League Baseball.

The Gators actually enjoyed better results in 1952. They won eight games. Florida capped its season with a 14–13 win over Tulsa in the Gator Bowl. That was Florida's first appearance in a bowl game. But that 1952 season would be the only standout year under Woodruff. He coached Florida

NEW PLACE TO PLAY

The Gators did not have a steady home during their early years. They played many home games at Fleming Field on their campus in Gainesville. But they also hosted opponents in Jacksonville, St. Petersburg, Tampa, and even Miami. That finally changed in 1930. A group led by University President John J. Tigert funded the construction of Florida Field. The facility opened on November 8. However, during its inaugural game, the Gators lost to Alabama 20–0 before 21,000 fans. To this day, Steve Spurrier–Florida Field at Ben Hill Griffin Stadium remains the team's home stadium.

✗ Coach Bob Woodruff, *third from left*, helped Florida improve, but he could not lead the Gators to a major title.

for 10 seasons. Yet only the 1952 squad won more than six games. Woodruff was fired after the 1959 season.

The bottom line was that Woodruff did not win enough games to save himself or his assistants. But that would not be a problem for Ray Graves. He replaced Woodruff as coach in 1960. And Graves was about to raise the Gators to new heights.

CHAPTER 3

PUTTING FLORIDA FOOTBALL ON THE MAP

Ray Graves took over as Florida's head football coach in 1960. He knew what he needed to win: better players. However, recruiting those players was easier said than done.

The Gators had been winners at times. But they had never contended for a national title. They had rarely even been a threat to win the SEC title. Graves was known as a great defensive coach from his time as an assistant with Georgia Tech. He also dumped the boring offense used by previous coach Bob Woodruff. Graves created an option attack. It gave the quarterback the choice of running or passing the ball. The offense also featured players in motion in hopes of confusing defenses.

Graves also wasted no time improving the Gators' defense. Florida ranked eleventh in the country in 1960 by allowing just

Florida coach Ray Graves installed an exciting offense upon arriving in 1960.

GATORADE

The popular drink Gatorade was created at the University of Florida and named after its sports teams. The football coaches asked a group of university doctors in 1965 why the heat was taking such a physical toll on the players. Later studies revealed that the players were losing fluids that were not being replaced. So the doctors created a new drink that would replenish what was lost during intense exercise. They named it "Gatorade."

The new drink was credited for keeping the players fresher than their opponents in 1965 and 1966. The result was nine victories and a spot in the Orange Bowl. Word of the new drink eventually spread to college football programs across the country. Gatorade was even said to have played a role in the success of the 1969 Kansas City Chiefs. The Chiefs upset the heavily favored Minnesota Vikings in the Super Bowl that season.

7.8 points per game. The team went 9–2 that season. It was the first time Florida had won nine games in a season. The Gators won their last four games, beating rival Georgia along the way. And Florida capped off the season with a 13–12 victory over Baylor in the Gator Bowl.

The coach had brought a sense of fun and achievement to his players. Quarterback Larry Libertore recalled how the new offense thrilled his teammates.

✕ **Florida star quarterback Steve Spurrier throws a pass against Georgia during his Heisman Trophy season of 1966.**

"I can remember in 1960 the look on the face of the players in the huddle of the excitement and the enthusiasm when I would call the play," Libertore said.

Florida fell to 4–5–1 the next year. But the squad continued improving after that. Florida finally had a top quarterback when star high school recruit Steve Spurrier took over the starting role in 1964. After a rocky first season, Spurrier passed for 3,905 yards and

30 touchdowns combined in 1965 and 1966. The Gators went 7–4 and then 9–2 in those years.

Florida was ranked among the top 10 teams in the country through most of those seasons. Spurrier was at his best as a senior in 1966, when he became the first Florida player to win the Heisman Trophy. The award is given annually to the best player in college football.

Spurrier led the Gators to their first Orange Bowl that season. The Orange Bowl is one of the most important bowl games each year. Florida faced off against Georgia Tech on January 2, 1967. A sore arm slowed down Spurrier. But sophomore halfback Larry Smith picked up the offense. He rushed for 187 yards. That included a 94-yard run. Meanwhile, the defense held the Georgia Tech quarterbacks to just eight completions in 22 attempts. Florida won the game 27–12.

After the game, Graves spoke about a new era of success for Gators football. "A lot of people wondered if Florida was a big enough team for this kind of a bowl game, and I think we showed we are," he said.

Spurrier was not able to bring Florida its first national title during his time there as a player. But the team was on the rise when he left. And the winning seasons continued in Gainesville. A trio of sophomores starred on the 1969 squad. They were quarterback John Reaves, wide receiver Carlos Alvarez, and future National Football League (NFL) superstar defensive end Jack Youngblood.

Together they stunned seventh-ranked Houston in the season opener. Then they won their next five games.

Florida soared to the seventh spot in the national rankings. But a midseason loss to Auburn and a tie against Georgia ended the Gators' national championship dreams. Reaves later said he thought his Gators should have finished the year unbeaten.

Reaves was not the only one who considered the 1969 season a disappointment. As such, Graves resigned to become the school's athletic director. He hired former Gators quarterback Doug Dickey to replace him. Dickey had just guided Tennessee to an SEC title. He could not do the same at Florida, though. He stayed at Florida for nine seasons, though his best finish was second place in the SEC in 1975.

Wide receiver Wes Chandler helped Florida to a strong three-year run surrounding that 1975 season. In 1974, the Gators sprinted to a 7–1 start and rose to number six in the national rankings. But they ended up finishing just 8–4 and losing to Nebraska in the Sugar Bowl. The 1975 squad went 9–3 but was shut out by Maryland in the

GREATEST GATOR DEFENDER?

Defensive end Jack Youngblood was one of the best defensive players in Florida history. He led the 1969 team with 66 tackles and earned All-America honors the following year. But Youngblood performed even better in the NFL. He played 14 seasons for the Los Angeles Rams. Youngblood earned a spot in the Pro Bowl every season from 1973 to 1979. He was inducted into the Pro Football Hall of Fame in 2001.

✖ **Florida wide receiver Cris Collinsworth caught 120 passes for 1,937 yards and 14 touchdowns from 1978 to 1980.**

Gator Bowl. Florida then went 8–4 in Chandler's junior season of 1976. However, at the Sun Bowl, Texas A&M handed Florida its fourth consecutive bowl loss.

Florida slipped to 6–4–1 in 1977 and 4–7 in 1978. Former Clemson coach Charley Pell replaced Dickey after that. But the coaching change did little to help the results on the field. Three early injuries destroyed Florida's 1979 season. Talented sophomore defensive lineman David Galloway was lost in the first game. All-America senior linebacker Scot Brantley and his brother, quarterback John Brantley, were injured in the second game.

The Gators never recovered. They finished 0-10-1. It was the first time the program failed to win a game since 1946.

"We never seemed to get a break," said junior quarterback Larry Ochab. "The ball always seemed to bounce against us."

Thanks to Pell, the ball would soon start bouncing their way. He worked to raise money and rebuild the entire football program. He improved the weight-training program. And he hired an assistant coach named Mike Shanahan, who would turn the Gators into an offensive power. The Gators were about to go from one of the worst teams in college football to one of the best.

COLLINSWORTH: WORTH PLENTY

Cris Collinsworth was recruited as a quarterback at Florida but was quickly moved to wide receiver. It turned out to be a good decision. Collinsworth caught 120 passes for 1,937 yards and 14 touchdowns from 1978 to 1980. And he just kept catching passes in the NFL. He had more than 1,000 receiving yards as a rookie with the Cincinnati Bengals. He matched the feat three more times in his career. Collinsworth also earned three trips to the Pro Bowl. He went on to become a popular NFL broadcaster.

CHAPTER 4

GRIDIRON GREATS IN GAINESVILLE

No college football team had ever sported a winless record one season and qualified for a bowl game the next season. That is, it hadn't happened until the Florida Gators did it in 1980.

Florida won six of its first seven games that season. That earned the Gators a spot in the top 20. The team eventually finished 8–4 after beating Maryland in the Tangerine Bowl. Behind a strong defense, Florida continued to improve in the years that followed. All-America linebacker Wilber Marshall led the way.

There was a problem, though. Florida was winning more games. But the Gators struggled to win big games. Florida started the 1983 season 6–0–1 and was ranked No. 5 in the nation. Then the Gators lost two in a row against fourth-ranked Auburn and fourth-ranked Georgia. Coach Charley Pell's days appeared numbered after that.

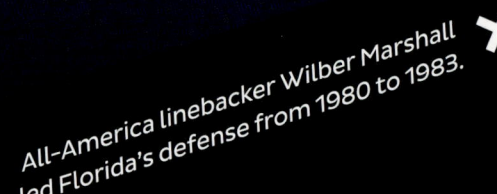
All-America linebacker Wilber Marshall led Florida's defense from 1980 to 1983.

TWO BACKS, ONE ROUND

In 1986 Florida's John L. Williams and Neal Anderson were taken in the first round of the NFL Draft. It marked the first time since 1971 that two running backs from the same school had been selected in the opening round. Anderson performed particularly well during his professional career. He recorded three 1,000-plus-yard seasons with the Chicago Bears.

Pell's fate was sealed early in 1984. The National Collegiate Athletic Association (NCAA) charged the program with 107 violations. The charges ranged from illegal recruiting practices to payment of athletes. The NCAA even charged Pell with spying on his SEC rivals. The Gators got off to a 1–1–1 start under Pell that season. Then he was fired and replaced by offensive coordinator Galen Hall.

Most people expected Florida to struggle in the wake of the violations. Instead, the 1984 squad became arguably the best Florida team to date. The Gators rolled over their next eight opponents. That included wins over eleventh-ranked Auburn, No. 8 Georgia, and twelfth-ranked Florida State.

With a 9–1–1 record, the Gators won their first SEC title. They climbed all the way up to number three in the nation. However, Florida was not allowed to play in a bowl game that year due to their NCAA violations. Then that spring, the SEC voted to void Florida's conference title. The conference also decided Florida would not be eligible to win the SEC title in 1985 or 1986.

✗ **Florida running back Emmitt Smith runs through defenders during a 1987 game against UCLA.**

Still, Florida won a lot of games, and many great players decided to play there in the years that followed. Among them was running back Emmitt Smith. As a freshman in 1987, Smith ran for 1,341 yards and 13 touchdowns. He averaged nearly six yards per carry. Smith peaked during his junior season with 1,599 rushing yards and 14 touchdowns. He was named SEC Player of the Year.

"I've been around a lot of great players, but (Smith) made unbelievable plays, and he made them look ordinary," Gators senior quarterback Kerwin Bell said in 1987. "Because Emmitt wasn't flashy at all. He had a great ability to make people miss him and also break tackles."

Smith was one of the best running backs in college football. But he could not turn the Gators into national championship contenders. They continued to have winning seasons. However, they never won quite enough to play in big-time bowl games.

The 1989 season was particularly rocky. The Gators started 4–1 under Hall. But the NCAA was preparing to punish Florida for illegal activities again. So Hall resigned, and the Gators finished 7–5.

The school hired its former Heisman Trophy winner, Steve Spurrier, to take over in 1990. But the new coach would have to work without Smith. The star running back decided to leave school early to enter the NFL Draft.

Even without Smith, the Gators improved in 1990. Spurrier developed a strong passing attack led by sophomore quarterback Shane Matthews. He threw for 2,952 yards and 23 touchdowns. The Gators scored at least 27 points in nine of their 11 games. Florida's 6–1 conference record would have won the SEC title. But the Gators were not eligible due to the NCAA violations.

Florida fans did not have to wait long to get that first official league title, though. The 1991 squad was the first in school history

✗ Florida quarterback Shane Matthews throws a pass during a 1992 game against Kentucky.

to win 10 games. And that year, Matthews won his second straight SEC Player of the Year Award.

The highlight of the year was a showdown against rival Florida State in the final regular-season game. One of Florida's touchdowns came on a 72-yard pass from Matthews to sophomore wide receiver

29

✕ **Florida players carry coach Steve Spurrier off the field after the Gators' victory over Alabama in the 1993 SEC title game.**

Harrison Houston. Meanwhile, Florida's defense stopped Florida State twice on the goal line. That helped the fifth-ranked Gators defeat the third-ranked Seminoles 14–9.

GREAT GATOR, GREATER COWBOY

Emmitt Smith blossomed into one of the top college football players at Florida. Few were surprised when he quickly became a star in the NFL. But Smith did much more than that. He went on to become one of the best running backs of all time. Smith was not particularly fast or strong. But he powered through holes and worked for every yard.

Sixteen picks were made in the 1990 NFL Draft before the Dallas Cowboys finally took him at number 17. They never regretted it. Smith was no doubt talented. But he also became known for his reliability and toughness. He set an NFL record by rushing for more than 1,000 yards for 11 straight years.

Smith led the league in rushing four times and in rushing touchdowns three times. He finished his career with a league-record 18,355 rushing yards. Smith was enshrined into the Pro Football Hall of Fame in 2010.

Florida moved up to number three in the country. However, the season ended on a sour note. Eighteenth-ranked Notre Dame upset Florida 39–28 in the Sugar Bowl. But it was hard for Florida fans to complain too much. Spurrier had turned the Gators into a national power. He had also helped clean up the program off the field.

The golden era of Gator football was just beginning. And the team's first national championship was right around the corner.

CHAPTER 5

THE CHAMPIONSHIP ERA

Coach Steve Spurrier had quickly turned Florida into one of the country's top programs. But untimely losses seemed to doom the team each season.

Several of those losses came against rival Florida State. Florida was 9–1 going into the 1993 showdown with Florida State. But the top-ranked Seminoles beat the seventh-ranked Gators 33–21. The rivals played twice in 1994. Florida was again 9–1 and ranked fourth when they met the first time. The seventh-ranked Seminoles pulled out a 31–31 tie. After Florida beat Alabama in the SEC Championship Game, the Gators and the Seminoles again met in the Sugar Bowl. Florida State came out on top this time, winning 23–17.

Florida finally got past Florida State in 1995. In fact, the Gators got past everybody during that regular season. Only one team

Florida quarterback Danny Wuerffel hurls a touchdown pass during a 1995 game against rival Florida State.

✗ **Florida wide receiver Ike Hilliard fights off two defenders during the 1997 Sugar Bowl against Florida State.**

was ranked higher than the undefeated Gators going into the bowl games. That was the Nebraska Cornhuskers, who thrashed Florida 62–24 in the Fiesta Bowl.

The 1995 season marked the closest Florida had been to winning a national title. The Gators then started the next season 10–0. But a loss to Florida State in the regular-season finale appeared to dash the Gators' national title hopes. That ended up not being the case, though. After beating Alabama again in the SEC title game, Florida got another crack at No. 1 Florida State in the Sugar Bowl.

This time, third-ranked Florida was ready. Senior quarterback Danny Wuerffel and junior wide receiver Ike Hilliard led the way. The pair connected seven times for 150 yards and three touchdowns. Florida held a seven-point lead at halftime. And the Gators then scored four unanswered touchdowns in the second half. The result was a 52–20 win. Florida had finally won its first national title.

Florida did not win another national title until 2006. But the Gators continued to be a force in college football. They won 29 of their next 34 games. They also were ranked in the top 10 nationally nearly every week for the rest of the decade.

Spurrier's coaching abilities had not gone unnoticed. The NFL came calling in 2002, when he left to coach the Washington Redskins. Former Florida assistant coach Ron Zook replaced him.

THE SPURRIER STORY

Steve Spurrier was known for his enthusiasm. Some believed he was immature and went overboard by yelling at referees. But there was no doubt that he had turned the Gators into a national power. His decision to leave Florida for the NFL didn't turn out as well as he'd hoped. Spurrier's Washington team went just 12–20 in two seasons. He then went back to college, coaching at South Carolina from 2005 to 2015. He coached the Gamecocks to an 86–49 record, including the program's first division title in 2010.

✗ Florida quarterback Tim Tebow gets high fives from fans after a 2007 game against Tennessee.

The Gators took a step back under Zook. They lost five games in each of his three years as coach. They also struggled to put away opponents. Florida blew fourth-quarter leads to Miami, Mississippi, and Florida State in 2003 and to Tennessee and Louisiana State University (LSU) in 2004. The last straw was an embarrassing loss to a 1–5 Mississippi State team midway through the 2004 schedule. Zook left at the end of that season.

Many Florida boosters hoped that Spurrier would return to save the program. Instead, Florida looked elsewhere. And the program would soon reach even greater heights.

Urban Meyer had just guided Utah to a 12–0 record. Several top football teams wanted to hire him. But Meyer decided to go to Florida. The school gave him a seven-year contract for $14 million. Florida fans hoped Meyer could bring top players and national titles back to Gainesville. And Meyer did both almost immediately. The Gators won their second national title after the 2006 season with the win over Ohio State.

The national title was a high point for the program. But the Gators would soon find even more success. Much of that was due to quarterback Tim Tebow. He had played a spot role in the national championship win as a freshman. After becoming the starter in 2007, Tebow blossomed into one of the greatest college football players ever.

Tebow passed and rushed for 42 total touchdowns in 2008. The offense also featured junior wide receiver Percy Harvin and sophomore center Maurkice Pouncey. Sophomore cornerback Joe Haden led the defense. All later became NFL standouts.

The Gators scored 45 points per game while winning the SEC title. They cruised through the regular season with an 11–1 record and then beat Alabama in the SEC Championship Game. That set up a showdown with Oklahoma in the BCS National Championship Game.

TALE OF TEBOW

In 2007 Florida quarterback Tim Tebow became the first sophomore to win the Heisman Trophy. As a Gator, he helped Florida win the 2006 and 2008 national titles. Many consider him to be one of the greatest college quarterbacks ever. Yet many experts questioned if Tebow would be a good NFL quarterback. Much of his college success was due to his rushing abilities. Professional quarterbacks do not run as often as college quarterbacks.

Still, the Denver Broncos selected Tebow in the first round of the 2010 NFL Draft. Tebow became the starter midway through his second season. And he started winning. The wins were not always pretty, but Tebow led the Broncos to the playoffs in 2011.

Regardless of his quarterbacking ability, there was no question Tebow was an amazing athlete. After his NFL career was over he decided to play minor league baseball. Tebow started in the lowest minor league level with the New York Mets organization in 2016, but by the end of the 2019 season he had earned promotion to their Triple-A team, one step from the major leagues.

The Sooners could not stop Tebow. He threw for 231 yards and ran for 109 more. He threw two touchdown passes, including one to junior wide receiver David Nelson with three minutes left that sealed the game. Harvin also starred in the 24–14 win. He combined for 171 total yards and added a touchdown.

Florida's defense played a big role in the win as well. Oklahoma had averaged 54 points per game that season. And the Sooners had scored more than 60 points in each of their previous five games. But Oklahoma's Heisman Trophy–winning quarterback, Sam Bradford, was held to just two touchdown passes that day. Meanwhile, Florida intercepted him twice.

Florida was the top-ranked team for much of Tebow's senior season in 2009. But Alabama bested the Gators in the SEC title game. Tebow still left on a high note with a 51–24 win over Cincinnati in the Sugar Bowl.

The Gators remained a strong team without Tebow—just not as strong. They finished 8–5 in 2010. Meyer then retired after that season to spend more time with his family.

Will Muschamp took over next. Muschamp had been the defensive coordinator for big programs such as Texas, LSU, and Auburn. After a 7–6 season in 2011, Muschamp had the Gators back to the level they hit under Meyer in 2012. Florida made the Sugar Bowl on the strength of a stout defense.

But it all fell apart in 2013. Florida lost its last seven games, including a loss to lower-division Georgia Southern. Florida finished 4–8 and missed a bowl for the first time in 23 years. When the outlook didn't improve in 2014, Muschamp was fired.

New coach Jim McElwain carried a reputation of building great offenses. That never occurred in Florida, but the team still won a lot of games. McElwain went 19–8 in his first two seasons. But McElwain clashed with Florida officials over the direction of the program.

✗ Backup quarterback Kyle Trask helped the Gators finish strong in 2019.

And after a 3–4 start to 2017, McElwain and the Gators agreed to part ways.

Florida wanted to get back to national title contention like they had when Tebow, Harvin, and other stars were in the lineup. Players like that were not easy to find, but they found the man who pulled the strings behind that offense. Dan Mullen was hired as head coach in 2018. Mullen had been the offensive coordinator under Meyer from 2005 to 2008.

Mullen engineered a big turnaround. Quarterback Feleipe Franks had yet to deliver on his promise in two years with Florida. But under Mullen he turned into one of the best quarterbacks in the SEC, leading the Gators to a 10–3 record and win in the Peach Bowl.

The next season, Franks dislocated his ankle early in the season, but backup Kyle Trask kept the Gators rolling. Trask threw for nearly 3,000 yards and 25 touchdowns in just 10 starts. And the Gators lost only two games. One was to eventual national champion LSU. The other was to Georgia, which also finished with a top-five ranking. Backed by the nation's seventh-rated defense, the Gators went 10–2 and then beat Virginia 36–28 in the Orange Bowl. In just his second year, Mullen had returned Florida to elite status among the nation's college football programs.

THE SWAMP

The Gators' home stadium is nicknamed "The Swamp." The name is a reference to the swampland in the Florida area. The stadium's official name was Florida Field until 1989. That is when Ben Hill Griffin's name was added to the mix. Ben Hill Griffin Jr. attended the school in the early 1930s. He gained tremendous wealth in the citrus, packaging, and cattle businesses and donated millions of dollars to the university. Steve Spurrier's name was added in 2016 for his own contributions to Florida. The stadium's official name became Steve Spurrier–Florida Field at Ben Hill Griffin Stadium.

TIMELINE

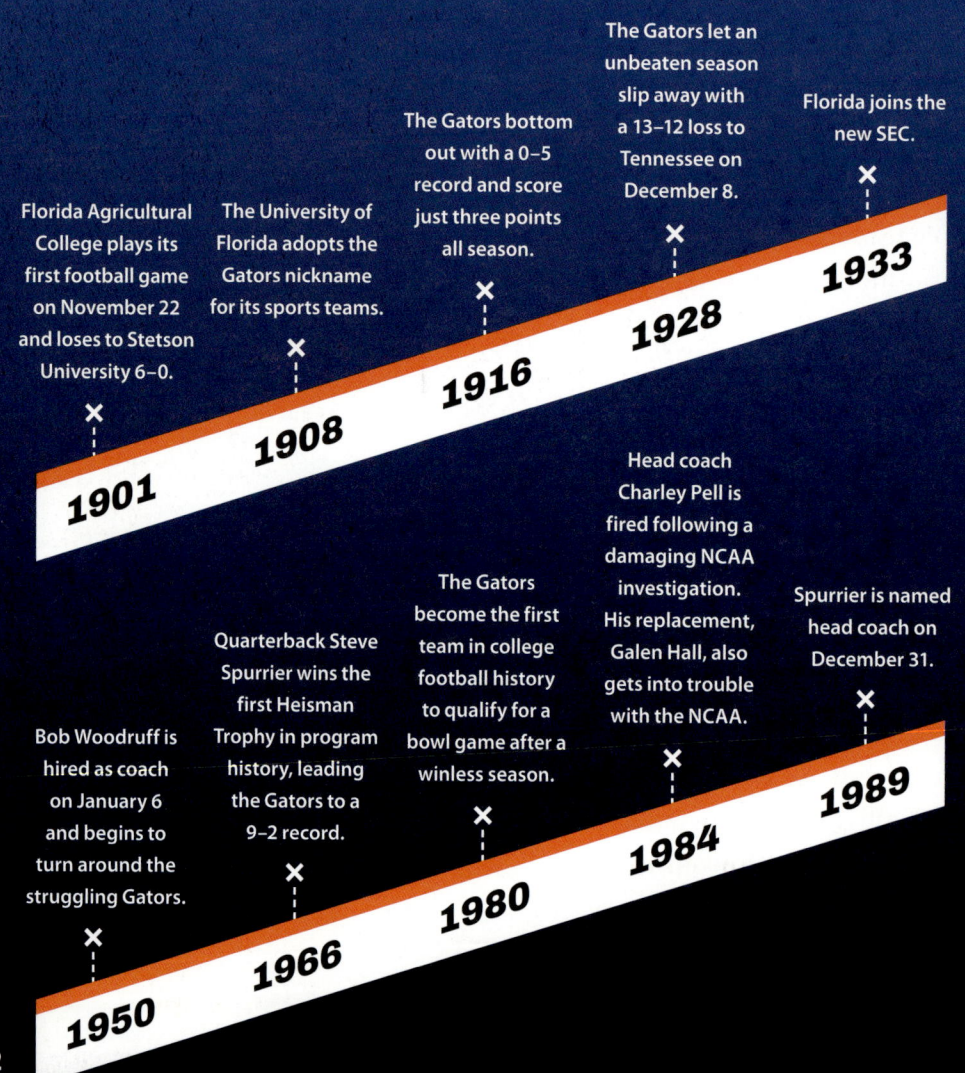

1901 — Florida Agricultural College plays its first football game on November 22 and loses to Stetson University 6–0.

1908 — The University of Florida adopts the Gators nickname for its sports teams.

1916 — The Gators bottom out with a 0–5 record and score just three points all season.

1928 — The Gators let an unbeaten season slip away with a 13–12 loss to Tennessee on December 8.

1933 — Florida joins the new SEC.

1950 — Bob Woodruff is hired as coach on January 6 and begins to turn around the struggling Gators.

1966 — Quarterback Steve Spurrier wins the first Heisman Trophy in program history, leading the Gators to a 9–2 record.

1980 — The Gators become the first team in college football history to qualify for a bowl game after a winless season.

1984 — Head coach Charley Pell is fired following a damaging NCAA investigation. His replacement, Galen Hall, also gets into trouble with the NCAA.

1989 — Spurrier is named head coach on December 31.

1996 — Quarterback Danny Wuerffel wins the second Heisman Trophy in Florida history.

1997 — Florida clinches its first national title on January 2 with a 52–20 defeat of Florida State in the Sugar Bowl.

2002 — Spurrier leaves as coach in January and is replaced by Ron Zook.

2004 — A bad loss to Mississippi State on October 23 leads to Zook's dismissal. Urban Meyer is named the new Florida coach on December 4.

2007 — Florida upsets Ohio State 41–14 in the BCS National Championship game on January 8.

2008 — Quarterback Tim Tebow wins the Heisman Trophy as Florida goes 13–1.

2009 — The Gators beat Oklahoma 24–14 on January 8 for their second national title in three years.

2013 — The Gators go 4–8 under third-year head coach Will Muschamp, missing a bowl game for the first time since 1990. Muschamp is fired the next year.

2018 — First-year coach Dan Mullen leads a revamped Florida offense to a 10–3 record including a win in the Peach Bowl.

2019 — The Gators go 11–2 and beat Virginia in the Orange Bowl.

QUICK STATS

PROGRAM INFO

Florida Agricultural College (1901–03)
University of Florida (1903–07)
University of Florida Gators (1908–)

NATIONAL CHAMPIONSHIPS

1996, 2006, 2008

OTHER ACHIEVEMENTS

SEC championships (1933–): 8
Division titles: 14
Bowl record: 23–21

KEY COACHES

Urban Meyer (2005–10)
   65–15, 5–1 (bowl games)
Steve Spurrier (1990–2001)
   122–27–1, 6–5 (bowl games)

KEY PLAYERS

Carlos Alvarez (WR, 1969–71)
Wes Chandler (WR, 1974–77)
Cris Collinsworth (WR, 1977–80)
Percy Harvin (WR, 2006–08)
Jevon Kearse (LB, 1996–98)
Charlie LaPradd (OL-DL, 1950–52)
Wilber Marshall (LB, 1980–83)
Emmitt Smith (RB, 1987–89)
Steve Spurrier (QB, 1964–66)*
Tim Tebow (QB, 2006–09)*
Dale Van Sickel (E, 1927–29)
Danny Wuerffel (QB, 1993–96)*
Jack Youngblood (DE, 1968–70)

HOME STADIUM

Steve Spurrier–Florida Field at
   Ben Hill Griffin Stadium (1930–)

*Heisman Trophy Winner
All statistics through 2019 season

QUOTES AND ANECDOTES

In December 1912, the Gators traveled to Cuba to play a game. When the officials failed to call a penalty, Florida coach G. E. Pyle angrily removed his team from the field. The Gators were forced to forfeit, and Pyle was arrested. The case never went to trial. Pyle and the Gators had to sneak out of the country by boat and sailed back to Florida.

In the early 1900s, the Gators played their home games at Fleming Field. The Florida baseball team and track-and-field squads also competed there. The football team played in front of fans sitting on the hoods of their cars parked along the sidelines.

Florida's most famous fan for 60 years was George Edmondson Jr. He was best known as "Mr. Two Bits" for a cheer he always started at home games. When Edmondson started attending games in the 1940s, "two bits" was slang for a quarter. His cheer went, "Two bits, four bits, six bits, a dollar, all for the Gators, stand up and holler!" Mr. Two Bits roamed section to section at games starting his cheer, always wearing khaki pants, a yellow dress shirt, and a necktie in Florida's orange and blue. Edmondson retired in 2008, but since then the university has chosen a celebrity or other fan to be the Honorary Mr. Two Bits at each game, wearing the familiar outfit and leading his favorite cheer. Edmondson died in 2019 at age 97.

"Call me arrogant, cocky, crybaby, whiner, or whatever names you like. At least they're not calling us losers anymore. If people like you too much, it's probably because they're beating you."

—Steve Spurrier, Florida's coach from 1990 to 2001

GLOSSARY

All-American
Designation for players chosen as the best amateurs in the country in a particular sport.

conference
A group of schools that join together to create a league for their sports teams.

contract
An agreement to play or coach for a certain team.

coordinator
An assistant coach who is in charge of the offense or defense.

dual threat
Very good at two different skills, such as running and receiving.

recruit
To convince a high school player to attend a certain college, usually to play sports.

retired
Ended one's career.

rival
An opponent with whom a player or team has a fierce and ongoing competition.

MORE INFORMATION

BOOKS

Campbell, Dave. *The Story of the Orange Bowl*. Minneapolis, MN: Abdo Publishing, 2016.

Wilner, Barry. *The Story of the College Football National Championship Game*. Minneapolis, MN: Abdo Publishing, 2016.

York, Andy. *Ultimate College Football Road Trip*. Minneapolis, MN: Abdo Publishing, 2019.

ONLINE RESOURCES

Booklinks NONFICTION NETWORK
FREE! ONLINE NONFICTION RESOURCES

To learn more about the Florida Gators, please visit **abdobooklinks.com** or scan this QR code. These links are routinely monitored and updated to provide the most current information available.

PLACES TO VISIT

College Football Hall of Fame
cfbhall.com

This hall of fame and museum in Atlanta, Georgia, highlights the greatest players and moments in the history of college football. Among the former Gators enshrined here are Jack Youngblood, Steve Spurrier, Wilber Marshall, and Emmitt Smith.

Steve Spurrier–Florida Field at Ben Hill Griffin Stadium
floridagators.com/facilities/ben-hill-griffin-stadium/1

Commonly known as "The Swamp," Ben Hill Griffin Stadium began as a simple 20,000-seat stadium in 1930 and now is one of the largest stadiums in college football, seating more than 88,000 fans.

INDEX

Alvarez, Carlos, 20
Anderson, Neal, 26

Bachman, Charlie, 13
Baker, Dallas, 7, 9
Bell, Kerwin, 28
Bradford, Sam, 39
Brantley, John, 23
Brantley, Scot, 23

Caldwell, Andre, 8
Chandler, Wes, 21
Collinsworth, Cris, 23

D'Agostino, Joe, 12
Dickey, Doug, 21–22

Franks, Feleipe, 41

Galloway, David, 23
Ginn, Ted, Jr., 7
Graves, Ray, 15, 16, 20–21

Haden, Joe, 37
Hall, Galen, 26, 28
Harvin, Percy, 7, 37–38, 40
Hilliard, Ike, 35
Houston, Harrison, 30

LaPradd, Charlie, 12
Leak, Chris, 7, 9
Libertore, Larry, 18–19

Marshall, Wilbur, 24
Matthews, Shane, 28–29
McElwain, Jim, 39–40
Meyer, Urban, 4–9, 37, 39
Moss, Jarvis, 7
Mullen, Dan, 41
Muschamp, Will, 39

Nelson, David, 38

Ochab, Larry, 23

Pell, Charley, 22–23, 24–26
Pouncey, Maurkice, 37

Reaves, John, 20–21

Shanahan, Mike, 23
Smith, Emmitt, 27–28, 31
Smith, Larry, 20
Smith, Troy, 7
Spurrier, Steve, 19–20, 28, 31, 32, 35, 37, 41
Sullivan, Haywood, 14

Tebow, Tim, 7–8, 37–40
Tigert, John J., 14
Trask, Kyle, 41

Van Sickel, Dale, 13

Warren, Fuller, 13
Williams, John L., 26
Woodruff, Bob, 12, 14–15, 16
Wuerffel, Danny, 35
Wynn, DeShawn, 7

Youngblood, Jack, 20, 21

Zook, Ron, 35–36

ABOUT THE AUTHOR

Tony Hunter is a writer from Castle Rock, Colorado. He lives with his daughter and his trusty Rottweiler, Dan.